SLOTH BEARS

by Tammy Gagne

AMICUS HIGH INTEREST ❖ AMICUS INK

Amicus High Interest and Amicus Ink
are imprints of Amicus
P.O. Box 1329, Mankato, MN 56002
www.amicuspublishing.us

Library of Congress Cataloging-in-Publication Data

Gagne, Tammy, author.
  Sloth bears / by Tammy Gagne.
     pages cm. -- (Wild bears)
  "Amicus High Interest is published by Amicus."
  Summary: "Presents information about sloth bears, their habitats in
the grasslands of India, and their unusual way of eating."-- Provided by
publisher.
  Audience: K to grade 3.
  Includes bibliographical references and index.
  ISBN 978-1-60753-777-9 (library binding)
  ISBN 978-1-60753-876-9 (ebook)
  ISBN 978-1-68152-028-5 (paperback)
  1. Sloth bear--Juvenile literature. [1. Bears.] I. Title.
  QL737.C27G325 2015
  599.78--dc23
                                2014043617

Photo Credits: gnagel/iStock/Thinkstock, cover; Brian Upton/Shutterstock
Images, 2, 13; Prashanth Nageshappa/Thinkstock, 4–5, 22; Animals
Animals/SuperStock, 6; Superstock/Alamy, 8–9; Ganesh H Shankar/Alamy,
10–11; Science Faction/SuperStock/Glow Images, 15; Joseph H. Bailey/
National Geographic Creative, 16; Danielrao/iStock/Thinkstock, 20–21;
Nagel Photography/Shutterstock Images, 19, 23

Produced for Amicus by The Peterson Publishing Company
and Red Line Editorial.

Designer Becky Daum
Printed in Malaysia

HC 10 9 8 7 6 5 4 3 2 1
PB 10 9 8 7 6 5 4 3 2 1

TABLE OF CONTENTS

Unusual Bears   4

Small, Shaggy Bears   6

Sloth Bear Senses   8

Digging for Food   10

Eating Bugs   12

A Sweet Tooth   14

Out and About   16

Sloth Bear Families   18

Bears in Danger   20

Sloth Bear Facts   22

Words to Know   23

Learn More   24

Index   24

UNUSUAL BEARS

Sloth bears have an unusual look. Their claws and fur make them look a bit like sloths. This is how they got their name. The bears live in forests and **grasslands**. They live mainly in India.

SMALL, SHAGGY BEARS

Sloth bears have **shaggy** black fur. They have white markings on their chests. They have long white snouts. Sloth bears grow up to 6 feet (1.8 m) long. This is smaller than other bears.

8

SLOTH BEAR SENSES

Sloth bears have small ears. They do not hear well. Their sight is weak. But they have great noses. They can smell food far away.

DIGGING FOR FOOD

Sloth bears eat **termites**. These insects live underground. Sloth bears dig to find the bugs. They use their curved claws.

Fun Fact
Sloth bears also eat fruit.

EATING BUGS

Sloth bears have a gap in their teeth. They suck up bugs through the gap. This is noisy. The bears can be heard far away.

A SWEET TOOTH

Sloth bears eat honey. They look for beehives in trees. Sloth bears are great climbers. They shake branches. They eat hives that fall.

Fun Fact
Sloth bears are also called honey bears.

OUT AND ABOUT

Sloth bears are awake at night. The darkness hides them from **predators**. Sloth bears find shelter in caves or trees when it rains.

Fun Fact
Tigers eat sloth bears.

SLOTH BEAR FAMILIES

Sloth bears have up to three cubs. Cubs live with their mother. Fathers do not help raise them. Cubs live alone after three years.

Fun Fact
Cubs ride on their mother's back.

BEARS IN DANGER

There are few sloth bears left. People have cleared many forests. Sloth bears have lost their homes. Today people are helping them. They create sloth bear **sanctuaries**.

21

SLOTH BEAR FACTS

Size: 121–308 pounds (55–140 kg), 60–75 inches (150–190 cm)

Range: India

Habitat: forests, grasslands

Number of babies: 1–3

Food: termites, fruit, honey

WORDS TO KNOW

grasslands – large, open, grassy areas

predators – things that hunt and eat other animals

sanctuaries – areas set aside for animals to live safely

shaggy – having long, messy hair

termites – insects that eat wood

LEARN MORE

Books

Brett, Jeannie. *Wild about Bears*. Watertown, Mass.: Charlesbridge, 2014.

Dolson, Sylvia. *Bear-ology: Fascinating Bear Facts, Tales & Trivia*. Masonville, Colo.: PixyJack Press, 2009.

Murray, Julie. *Sloth Bears*. Edina, Minn.: Big Buddy Books, 2013.

Websites

National Geographic—Sloth Bears
http://animals.nationalgeographic.com/animals/mammals/sloth-bear
Learn more about the sloth bear's unusual way of eating.

San Diego Zoo—Sloth Bears
http://animals.sandiegozoo.org/animals/sloth-bear
See more sloth bear photos and find more fun facts about them.

INDEX

appearance, 4

claws, 4, 10
climbing, 14
cubs, 18

fur, 4, 7

habitats, 4, 21
honey, 14

insects, 10, 12

predators, 17

sanctuaries, 21
senses, 9
size, 7